No Dead Beat Jobs

7 Reasons Why It's Time To Start Thinking About A Career Change

Transition from your job to a career that you love within 6 to 12 months

Eyedentified Consulting Services, LLC
d/b/a Eyedentified Publishing Solutions
P.O. Box 6892
Springdale, AR 72766-6892
www.eyedentifiedconsulting.com

Publisher's Note: Any resemblance to names, characters, places, incidents, actual people, living or dead, or to businesses, companies, events, institutions, or locales is completely coincidental.

Book Layout & Design © 2019 Show Your Success Co.
No Dead Beat Jobs/ LaTonya R. Jackson. -- 1st ed.
Library of Congress Control Number: 2019904574
ISBN 978-1-9455661-0-3 (trade paper)

Dedication

To Maurice, Sydni, Josiah, and Nathaniel - Thank you for allowing me to grow as I learned to move beyond the history that informed who I was to become who I am. Today, I am defined by my unique gift mix and who I have always been created to be. Let that always be our legacy.

Be who you are always and let no person or thing keep you from fulfilling your functional assignment in the earth "…for your Father [Abba] knows the things you have need of before you ask Him." ~Matthew 6:8 NKJV

Table of Contents

Acknowledgments

Special thanks to those who supported this book:

- Missy Washam
- Anthony "Tony" Richardson
- Jason & Jessica Watson
- Brenda Deal
- Naomia Rivera
- Natasha "Tasha" Sarver
- Albert & Deborah Floyd
- J. Gabriela "Gaby" Garcia
- Greg Smith
- Jamie Maestri
- Deven Chambers
- Aarthi Janakiraman
- Willa Ball
- Kennetra Smith
- Jessica Thompson
- Donald & Tammy Johnston
- Todd & Autumn Murner
- Beatrice Floyd
- Wesley "Wes" Kawata
- Nathan and Carrie Nichols
- Connie Kelley

Introduction

WELCOME TO NO DEAD-BEAT JOBS: 7 REASONS WHY IT'S Important to Start to Make a Career Change! I am excited that you have decided to take a look at this excellent work (yes, I'm a little biased) and that you found value in picking it up and desire to read it. In so doing, you will find tips, tools, and resources to enable you toward a successful transition on your next career journey.

Why is this book important? Well today, we often hear individuals talk about being careful not to get into a dead-end job. I purposely chose to use different language because we want neither a dead-end nor a dead-beat job. So what exactly is a dead-end job? A dead-end job is a job in which there's no chance of advancing to a higher level role or a better job. It is also defined as a job that we find ourselves in that we chose to settle for which has no end in sight and offers minimal value or growth for you. It's all about a job, a position not offering an opportunity for you to improve your situation or to express your value, or your unique gift mix versus a career. A career, in my mind, is a position in which the work brings fulfillment and joy, and something you love to do every day. It answers the question of, "What do I want to be when I grow up?" and "What do I want to do when I grow up?" Many of us couldn't answer that question when we were younger, and some of us can't answer that question today.

This book is going to help walk you through a process that's going to help you answer the question of who you want to be when you grow up and what you want to do. It's going to help you discover how to leverage who you already are, the innate abilities, skills, and knowledge you've acquired from your years of living and experience and things to which you've been exposed. It's going to help you take your years of investing and acquiring knowledge and craft that unique gift mix that can lead you to a place of career or life fulfillment.

Here's how this book came to be: I began my career search journey at an early age. I've been working since I was 14 years old. I started as a food service worker at a local hospital in Nebraska. My mom was a single mother, she had a stroke, and we were in a detrimental financial situation. However, my mom had a vast support network because she doesn't meet a stranger. As a result of that, some people came into my life who are still part of my life today.

One of them was a woman. She was my hair stylist and a single mom who had her own business. She had a home and was living life and loving the life she lived. I kept thinking, how in the world does she do that? How can I ever live the life I want to live?

I dismissed that thought for many years and went to work in corporate America. My goal was to be the CEO of a Fortune 500 company. That was my dream based on an assignment I forgot to do during my senior year and had five minutes to complete.

As an undergraduate student, I was a marketing and finance major. I loved business. I went into the corporate environment, and lo and behold! I was doing marketing for a company, and I didn't enjoy it. So I went back to school and got a Master's Degree in higher education leadership. I was talking with a faculty member who was one of my advisors. He looked at me one day and said, "Why are you in education? Ever since I met you, you should be in corporate America." He was right. I was sort of yearning for more excitement, more adventure, and higher education wasn't fulfilling to me at that time.

So I went back into a corporate environment and took an internship in market research. I loved it, but the company went through a round of layoffs.

So there I was, an intern who'd only been on the job for seven months and the company began laying people off. I was blessed and grateful that I was not laid off at that moment. There was a glass wall, and I remember watching folks walk with their life, their work life in a box. I could see the tears on their faces. I remember thinking, "Wow, why would a company ever do that? Lord, I hope I'm never that person."

Fast forward to when I'm working in human resources with another company. I finally found the area I loved. I love strategy and strategic thinking. I love helping people think through processes, systems, and structures among other things. I had been on maternity leave and returned to work, and could feel there was a pause in the air. People were more stressed than usual, and I knew what was coming. Here I was clear for the first time on what I loved and yet perplexed about what path to take given the impending news. So I did what any "normal" person would do, right? No! I went to my boss a couple of weeks before Oct. 2, 2015, and said, "I know what's coming. I know we're about to go through layoffs. If you need someone on our team to take the hit, I'm willing to be your person."

Now I did that full of faith, full of spiritual acuity that it was the right move to put my position and myself on the line. Oct. 1, I received the meeting planner notification, and at 8 a.m. on Oct. 2, I had the meeting – my position was eliminated.

I was offered another job, but I had three days to make a decision. Do I take that job and stay, or do I walk away and do something I've wanted to do for a very long time – pursue entrepreneurship full-time? I have been doing business on the side for years. I've done network marketing businesses, helped with resume writing, assisted with interviewing skills, conducting mock interviews with people, taught motivational speaking classes and just really honed in on what I love to do, and what I liked or didn't like about it. Each of those environments was preparing me for the next assignment.

So finally, here's the door. In the three days, I discussed it with my family, consulted with our spiritual leaders, and ultimately a decision had to be made – I chose to walk away. That first year was challenging. I didn't have much business. People I had in my network threw me a bone here and there, and those bones began to lead to skeletons of projects and ultimately full-on projects. As a result of that, here I am three years later, writing a book and telling my story to you.

I want you to be clear about who you are. I want you to be clear about what you bring to the table. I want you to be able to articulate your position succinctly. I want you to build your network well. And I want you to leverage every opportunity in your current environment to develop the skills necessary to be able to step out fully assured and full of faith that this thing you have, this unique gift mix, is what's going to help you to build and establish whatever you choose for your life.

Whether it's transitioning into a career that you love or starting a business, it will likely lead to a better, more important and engaging aspect of daily life and living. The choice may help you improve your situation and not feel stuck in a dead-end or a dead-beat job; rather, it will allow you to the opportunity to decide to step into a fulfilling, loving, holistic career you've created. Why? Because you are a holistic person, and you've chosen to invest in what's necessary today that will help lead you to success tomorrow.

You Must Know Who You Are

"There's no greater gift you can give and receive than to honor your calling. It's why you were born and how you become truly alive."

— OPRAH WINFREY

THIS CHAPTER IS ALL ABOUT YOU! IT'S ABOUT YOU ENHANCING your self-awareness. It's about you recognizing who you are and how who you can translate your gifts and uniqueness to pursue a career or a business opportunity that can bring profitability to you and your family. It's about getting rid of stinking thinking. It's about finding a place that's going to bring fulfillment into your life and the value you're going to be able to deliver, not just to yourself but to those who are going to benefit from you operating and functioning in who your unique gift mix. You'll be able to help others function in who their unique gift mix because you'll be in the right position, at the right time and in the right place to be able to help them be in their correct position. Your positioning will then help them to propel beyond who they could ever have become without your presence (your book, career taking on a leadership role, starting your business, etc.) in their life. So stop the B.S. (Bogus Stories) that hinder your genius and brilliance. Limiting beliefs come from the B.S. we tell ourselves about who we are and what we are not capable of doing. Instead of that approach, embrace the REAL you, discover your why, design your life, develop your craft and deliver all with excellence.

What is Your Why?

Oprah Winfrey said, "There's no greater gift you can give and receive than to honor your calling. It's why you were born and how you become truly alive."

Do you want to become truly alive? Do you desire to honor your calling? Think about your why. Who were you born to be? It's a different question than what you want to do; it's about the calling you have upon your life and how you honor that calling by what you choose to do in your career. I know, it's hard. Most of us lose time trying to figure out why we exist, our purpose or our function in the earth. Others wake up with a clear vision of what they are meant to do. This concept is not something we can explain easily, and yet it is necessary to finding fulfillment in any aspect of our lives. Our "why" is unique and differs for every one of us.

My why will be different from yours, and *your* why will be different from your neighbors', or even from your sibling. Because it is *your* why – no one else is called to do what you do, how you will do it in the earth. It's your functional fingerprint or what makes you uniquely you.

In simple terms, *your* why or purpose or calling is the reason you exist and the reason you choose to get up every morning and engage with life. No, you don't get up because you have to go to work so you can pay your mortgage or other bills. It's not even about safety, security and the financial aspect of things, or being able to spend time with your family. It goes much deeper than that.

What is your reason for getting up in the morning? It may be because you're helping six-year-olds learn to read or write or add. It could be that you love helping people figure out who they are so they can live a life that's full of purpose and passion, and it's fulfilling for them. Maybe it is so you can put food on the table for your family and have a flexible enough schedule so you can volunteer at your favorite charity or be home with your kids after school and teach them how to do other things like gardening, or cutting the grass. It's the thing that provides energy, excitement, and reinvigorates you no matter the challenge you face. It's what keeps you going. You would do this calling for FREE and even find ways to embed it into your daily life as an occupational hobby (the job you do that's not in your job description or the other duties as assigned).

So what gives you a sense of fulfillment and happiness when you do it? Whatever that is for you, that is what is essential, and it's what makes your why vital. These examples are things we choose to do without getting paid. It is imperative you do what your calling or purpose is in life. It's the thing that might have no financial reward. It's the thing that's going to reward you innately, bring you great fulfillment in life and help you experience joy with activities and better connect with those who are around you. That's *your* why!

Repurpose Your Purpose

When you know what you like to do and you're doing it, you're willing to do that without being paid. Repurposing your purpose is taking the thing you love to do and ensuring that you're able to do it the way you want to do it. If it's writing songs and releasing them to the masses, but it's not edifying to you, then why do it the way the "world" says that you should to achieve success? What if you feel your calling is to rear happy or healthy kids? How do you create an environment where you can raise happy and healthy kids and do what you love? Perhaps this means that one person stays at home and the other works outside the home, or has a work-from-home opportunity. Maybe you're a single parent, and you need to work and be able to bring home the bacon, cook the bacon and provide that bacon to your children. How can you do that in such a way where you're doing what you love, and you're allowing yourself to be compensated for it and compensated handsomely?

Everyone is capable of being compensated for what they do when they do what they love. Not everyone chooses to engage that, especially when uncertain of how you could be living a life less than who you should be versus living in the overflow and abundance of joy, peace, and fulfillment in all that your hand touches.

Repurposing your purpose is all about choosing how you're going to engage with your *why* and then leveraging it to bring wealth, health and a love for life into your daily agenda. It means being compensated; whether you're working for somebody else or working for yourself – which is my preference – to be able to leverage that purpose to bring fulfillment, joy, and happiness to the life you're called to live.

Make a Decision to Change

In January 2019, I participated in a four-week course entitled *SoulShift* with Shun Strickland. The focus of the course was the concept of moving away from a soul search to making a soul shift, which required me to make an intentional decision to align my soul (mind, will, emotions, intellect, and imagination) with who I believe I am called and uniquely gifted and purposed to be. One of the questions asked during that class was, "Now what?" Now that you know who you are, you know what your calling is, and you have repurposed your purpose, it's time to make a decision. You've got to take action. Taking action requires you to make a series of conscious choices that allow you to progress into who you desire to be. In other words – DECIDE!

Let's begin with the first letter in decide. The letter D represents the discovery process. **Discover** your brilliance. We began our discussion in this chapter about examining the importance of your why, your calling or purpose. Waiting to be unearthed in each of us is our unique gift mix. It is crying out for us to harness and stand in our respective power. The unique aspect of this gift mix leads to purposeful living, not only for you but for those around you.

The second letter in the acronym DECIDE is E, which urges you to **Encourage** yourself. In the Bible, there's a story of a king named David, who faced many challenges and opposition. David lamented that even amid the most difficult or trying times he would have to encourage himself. I recognize that from my own experiences and believe it will resonate with you, that when it feels like nobody will support you for the direction you've chosen to walk in your life, you will need to have ways to encourage yourself without needing others to be available to you or requiring them to do this for you.

The third letter is C – Commit! Make a **Commitment**; commit your life to change. You may find you have to make a conscious choice to sit down and commit your life to the direction you want to take instead of allowing yourself to continue making excuses as to why your life can't move forward. I had to do the same. Getting rid of the B.S. (Bogus Stories) in my mind was no easy task. Stop making excuses for why you can't move your life forward and do the work required to change.

The I in DECIDE is **Invite truth.** You must allow yourself to invite truth in, whether that truth comes from within or an external source. In most cases, if you've been lying to yourself on the inside, the truth is going to have to come from elsewhere, but you've got to be open enough to receive it. And the first way to open yourself is to invite truth into you. And once you invite truth in, you can have a more clear why. One way to combat lies and bogus stories we've told ourselves is to speak or write down the opposite of what we currently believe. Then begin to say aloud the truthful statement each time resistance is present resultant from the B.S. in your mind.

The last D is to **Determine** the way forward. You can be more clear about how you're going to move forward in the direction of the *why* you've established for yourself if you've allowed yourself to create a plan for how you are going to achieve your desired outcome. Allow flexibility within the framework of the plan, but a plan needs to be present to help posture you for the position you hold as a promise within your heart. Once you start in a direction, you will have commenced the journey that will take you to a destination. Failure to determine the direction you wish to go only fuels the B.S. that exists in your mind. Capture in writing the steps you intend to take to move beyond your present situation, and you will be one step closer to arriving at your destination.

And last but not least, you're going to E, **Evict** B.S. and wrong thinking forever. You've discovered your brilliance. You've encouraged yourself. You've committed your life to change. You've invited truth to come in. You're now clear enough to determine which way you want to go. You've got to evict any wrong thinking or any opportunity for wrong thinking to come into your mind to hinder you or to take you back to a place of perceived safety or security for your life. The pursuit of your purpose and calling may require risks; if you desire to move forward in a career or business, you are going to have to take a risk and trust yourself in the journey. It's not going to necessarily be easy to make that final decision if your thinking is incorrect and if the way you're processing information doesn't align with your *why* and the purpose and goal that you've established from the beginning.

Let Go of Fear & Offense

Transitioning from my career was a huge risk for me. I made a six-figure income apart from my spouse with two children, a mortgage and other responsibilities. I knew within myself it was the right move at the moment. I stepped outside of what was comfortable and familiar to step into what was uncomfortable and unfamiliar. When I did, fear tried to set itself within me. Fear might also occur as you pursue your calling. You may DECIDE to take that risk; often, you'll step out and fear will try to grip you. I learned a long time ago that fear is simply false evidence that appears to be real. We've all heard that. The concept of fear lacks any substance to yield fruit except that which we feed it. In other words, we provide the fuel as evidence to aggregate a real presence of something that cannot exist apart from our engagement. It's air – blow out the exhaust and blow it away. What are those thoughts? Thoughts that you can't make it. Financially, things might start to shift, or you might step into a new work environment questioning whether or not you're qualified. You're trying to figure out if you have to prove yourself. Or when you feel like you have to overachieve to show the people who hired you that they made the right decision. And all of that is fear based. Fear-based decisions originated from fear-based thoughts.

Let go of that fear on the inside so you can enjoy the process and the journey you're walking toward and moving forward in.

As you release fear, you may find you also have to release yourself from being offended. Ironically, it was Oct. 1, 2017, (recall just two years earlier that I took the risk to step out into my dream), and I was having shoulder stress and neck pain. There was a constant knot in my left shoulder that would temporarily be relieved upon an alignment of the C2, 3 or 4 vertebrae (I saw a chiropractor). And I remember the day I let go of offense. In my personal life, I was praying, and as a result of that, I was listening to someone who was teaching about letting go the root of offense and where it resonates within the body, and I began to weep uncontrollably. At the moment, I realized that I had somewhere along the journey become offended by my former employer. I also recognized I had become offended by my life. I had become offended with how things had worked out because they didn't meet my expectations.

When life doesn't meet your expectations, or you have unrealized or unspoken expectations out there, nobody knows about them, and they're not being fulfilled *because* no one knows about them. Becoming offended can create physical and emotional challenges, and can hurt and hinder relationships. I released offense that day and never looked back. The result of letting go of offense is a new perspective and outlook that focuses on your desired position and outcomes and allows you to freely move forward into an upright posture that is not slumped over like a wind-up dead-beat person slothing through life.

You've got to let go of the offense in order to receive what you need to be successful. And when you let go of fear and offense, you're going to step out into the next place that's going to help you to be successful in the way you desire to be.

Make Sure Your Family Knows and Is On Board

Once you've discovered who you are, why you believe you exist and what your unique contributions are in the world, and you've repurposed that so you can leverage it to bring in income, you've made a conscious decision to move forward and you've let go of the fear and the offense emotions. Now your family is going to start to see you change.

As you change, the family needs to know why you're changing, why you've come to this place, and who this new person is you are becoming. They need to know how they still fit into your life, your vision and dreams, and their part within it. The family also needs to know how they can help you to move forward in your unique gift mix or calling now that you are certain you want to go after it.

As a result of that conversation, you want to ensure they agree with you, that they're on board with that direction to shift and change. This conversation is necessary before you go out and make any adjustments. You want to find that place of agreement. You want to make a decision together on how you're going to move forward taking into account the impact on your family, your spouse, your children or others of significance in your life. Your time is also going to be a factor because maybe you are working full-time currently and you're going to begin to pursue that which you know you should be doing if it aligns to your life. There might be some additional time required in the evenings or on weekends for you to take a class and go to school, or connect with a coach who might require some financial resources.

No matter the desired outcome, you want to make sure you are in alignment on how you're going to move your dream forward and how you're going to work together as a family, and that they're on board with the plan so you can achieve what you set out to accomplish.

Be Accountable

Being accountable is, in my opinion, having someone who's going to hold your feet to the fire if you will. Hold your feet to the fire meaning that once you put this out there to your family and maybe even to a few close friends, they're not going to reject you in any way, but going to become your support system. They're your trusted advisors on this journey.

And as a result, they're also going to be the people who have a responsibility for you accomplishing that which you set out to accomplish. That's accountability.

So when you say, "I'm going to write a book," for example, your team of trusted advisors is going to say, "How's your book coming?" They're going to ask you questions. They're going to check in on you to see how you're progressing against the plan you're going to create to achieve your dream.

Accountability is for you! Although we want you to let go of fear and offense, and we want you to omit wrong thinking as part of making your decision, there are going to be moments where you might find yourself questioning the decisions you make. And that team of people, your support system you have around you is going to be there to reinforce what you told them was the goal and the outcome you set at the beginning of the journey.

Let's say your goal is to write a book in 30 days. Your support structure or team of trusted advisors is going to ensure you are equipped to write that book in 30 days. They will check in on you and remind you of the goal or the words that you spoke over yourself about how you were going to achieve that particular dream as you pursue your goal. They will like and share your progress and completed work. They will purchase the book to ensure your endeavor is successful based on your definition of success. They will guard you and help you guard against yourself during the timeframe you established to achieve what you set out to achieve, whether in your career or a business environment.

You Must Know What You Like to Do

"Success is liking yourself, liking what you do, and liking how you do it."

—MAYA ANGELOU

KNOWING WHAT YOU LIKE TO DO IS ALL ABOUT IDENTIFYING and solidifying your strengths by looking at yourself holistically. That's taking 360-degree views of you and focusing on the areas that align with the vision you have for yourself, your career and your life. And each one of those things might look slightly different because vision isn't limited in its scope or expression. You don't have to have one singular vision for your entire existence. You can have a vision for each area of your life – your health, your family and your career.

You'll want to look at the vision for your career holistically. You may choose to recognize that being able to have the vision for your career requires a holistic picture of who you are, how you're going to function and in what areas you function best. It's going to enable you to be more successful in your career because you're sure of what you bring to the table.

What Are Strengths?

There are a lot of tools available in the marketplace for you to be able to identify your strengths. Let's start with knowing where your strengths, interests, and hobbies are to begin to gain clarity on what you like to do. So, what do you like to do? Where do you find that you gain energy when you engage in a particular activity or a particular service? Who is around when you do that? How do you feel when you're around those people? When you're engaged in that activity? What do you feel when you do those activities? What are your strengths? What are the strengths you have that maybe even in your life over time are threaded or thematic? What have you heard from others who have supported you? What do you like about your job? What don't you like? I know that's a lot of questions, but it is in those questions we will find the answers we seek.

Whether it is strong at giving details or great at taking care of kids, you might be amazing at creating things whether that means designing a display case or creating content, physical crafts or messages that inspire emotions in people. Whatever that is for you, 9 out of 10 times you're already doing it. You may not consciously be aware of it. Begin to journal about what you're good at, what you like about what you do and then DO IT! At least for a day or two, to begin to make the comparison. The goal here is to identify the thing you like to do and leverage that as an area of strength for your life; an area of strength you can then utilize to propel you forward faster.

How do you add value?

You begin to add value by first seeing the value in others. Seeing the value in others goes beyond the surface relationships of being acquainted with someone. It is about identifying and recognizing the unique contribution and benefit of being in the presence of another. In so doing, there is then that conviction within the heart to add value to a person because of the potential of participating in their journey to help them uncover and unveil who they were always meant to become.

As you consider the organization you're a part of, do you say, "I am here to add value to this company," or "I am here to add value to this relationship?" It is producing beyond the expectation to create and yield impact in your life and the lives of those around you. Ask yourself this: When people come into your presence, are they left with an emotional wake because you spewed your complaints, dislikes or gossip on them, leaving them run down and feeling run over? Or are they leaving your presence feeling like there's hope, joy and opportunity to move forward in life after having been built up again? To add value, you should leave those you encounter, inclusive of the entities within which you work, in a state that's better than it was when you weren't present or part of it. Do it in the way that allows you to remain true to your beliefs and values, to be able to move forward past anything that could be a hindrance or a blockage. Be the person who brings an increased perspective or presence to any person or entity as a result of your presence, and the value you bring through your expression will yield dividends that a job can't provide.

Identify Your Pros and Cons

In any experience you've had, you may find aspects of various activities that you liked and things you didn't like.

Let's start this process by reviewing the past ten years of life. Expand the timeline until you can no longer find congruence in what you see as a thread of what you like to do versus what you don't like to do. Think of the life you've lived across the recommended expanse of time. Take the time to make a list of the things you enjoyed about activities you engaged in while in school, on the job or within the community, etc. Now look at the same list and identify the things you didn't like, or the cons for each environment you listed. Compare the pros and cons. This list is not exhaustive and is only reflective based on where you are today in your growth journey. As you grow and change in life, you may find that what you liked in one era of your life is completely different from another era.

What are the things you did? What did you like about them? What didn't you like? Personally, professionally, as a volunteer, roles you had as a mom, wife, dad, husband, boss, leader, manager or as a subordinate. Review the activities holistically, looking at them from all angles to ensure you capture your likes and dislikes as accurately as possible. Once your list is complete, highlight all the strengths for you that align to the person you set out to become.

Conduct a Personality Assessment

There are ample personality assessments in the marketplace, and I can connect you with different ones. There's the DiSC profile, Birkman Method, the Myers-Briggs Type Indicator, StrengthsFinder, Enneagram, Fascinate Advantage Assessment and more. There are so many different resources available to help you with your discovery journey. These are all tools that can give you insight into the things you like to do and the things that you don't like to do as they relate to your life, and an insight into your strengths and growth opportunities. Some may also be able to tell you where your interests lie because maybe you haven't articulated something very clearly and you don't realize you have a natural affinity toward a particular task or action.

The resources available are designed to help you look at yourself and bring a greater level of self-awareness. When you do that, you're going to be able to have some evidence-sharing support to bring a balance of perspective to the things you've identified. This expression will include use of the tools we previously talked about by identifying your strengths and looking at how you add value for yourself and others and then looking at your pros and cons list. The personality assessment you choose should be a confirmation of what you already know about yourself. It should also give you language you can use to talk about how those strengths will help you as you go about making a career transition and then leveraging that information to get your resume updated and reflective of the strengths you possess.

A personality assessment will also help you begin to articulate what you like and don't like to do as you progress toward a vision and dream you have for your career.

Talk to Other People

I recommend individuals complete a 360-degree assessment, herein referred to as 360, in professional and personal life. It's not necessarily a personality assessment but more a tool that is going to give you insight from others about yourself, your strengths, blind spots, areas of growth and opportunities. You can do a 360 without having a formalized process, and what I mean by that is, you can choose to talk to other people, right?

A 360 involves self-evaluation. You've already done some of that if you followed the steps and recommendations

I made in Chapter 1 and have been following along so far in Chapter 2.

You also then hopefully have someone you have reported to in the past or you are currently reporting to who can provide feedback on how you are performing and what strengths they see in you, where they see some blind spots and even some areas of opportunity for growth.

Beyond that, you also want to talk with your peers. If you volunteer at your church or your community; you sit on a board. You'll want to talk to those alongside you to get their feedback on how you work. You might say, "Hey, I'm just doing some self-evaluation. I want to understand. I'm looking at my strengths, blind spots and growth areas. What feedback would you like to share with me? Is there anything you see that I need to do differently?"

The goal is to have conversations with people who are at an equal level with you through a working relationship. If you have individuals who "report" up to you, you also want to get their engagement through this process.

This process is not limited to a corporate or professional relationship. You might consider talking with the most honest people in the world – your children (or someone else's) – to get feedback. I like to use children because they're so honest. They're not going to hold back their words. (At least my kids don't.) So I'll say, "How did mommy respond? Did I respond right in that situation? What do you think?"

And my child will say, "No, mom. You were mean." Or, "That wasn't very nice or kind. Your words kind of hurt. You could have said it differently." And so by getting that 360-degree perspective, you get a holistic picture of who you are and how it's playing out in your day-to-day activities and life. Gaining a perspective that's not your own in an objective manner from those who have an affinity toward you and those who do not can eliminate your self-bias and allow you to see a full picture of how you're viewed by those around you.

Follow Your Gut

After you've done all these things, you've identified your strength. You've looked at how you add value for yourself and others examined your pros and cons, taken a personality assessment or two, completed a 360 and talked to other people. You've got your *why*, and it's clear. You know your purpose, and you looked at how you can repurpose it. At the end of the day, whatever direction you consciously decide, you've got to do the thing that feels right to you.

I was on a coaching call with someone, and the individual kept telling me about everybody else. And anytime I asked the individual the question, "What makes you happy? What do you want?" The person would deflect. "The writers on my team do this," or, "You know what? There's a selfish person in my organization that just really, takes over the meeting."

And I sat there thinking, "Why are you talking to me about everybody else? What do *you* want?" And part of that goes back to why it's important to let go of fear. The other part of that is the person just has to acknowledge what drives their behavior.

We got to the point of saying, "Listen, at the end of the day if the company doesn't give you what you want and don't give you the job you're seeking, if they don't help to bring you to that career place that's part of your plan, what decision are you going to make?" And I said, "But you've got to do what feels right to you. I can't make that decision for you. Neither can your spouse, your parents, your children – no one in the world. It is a decision you'll have to make, and you'll want to be equipped and ready to make that decision.

Given the vast list of resources available, I caution against getting analysis paralysis. Don't second-guess yourself. You've got to listen to the inner witness that will guide your journey toward one that is fulfilling and leading to love instead of lies and limitations. As you listen to the inner witness, you will discover what you want to do. This is what you want to pursue. And therefore, you decide by following your gut and doing the thing that feels right to you. No one else can do that for you.

If all the personality assessments say you should be a financial analyst, but your gut says you should be a creative designer, then follow your gut because that's what's going to lead you to fulfillment and happiness as you transition your career or into business, whatever you've chosen to do.

Conduct Informational Interviews

"Every great dream begins with a dreamer. Always remember, you have within you the strength, the patience, and the passion to reach for the stars to change the world."

—HARRIET TUBMAN

EVERYTHING YOU NEED IS WITHIN YOU! IT'S TIME TO GATHER information for the dream, for the career, or the opportunity you've expressed interest in that's going to help you to find fulfillment in the purpose and life you've chosen to live for yourself, that one that links to your *why*.

The informational interview is a process where you step out of your comfort zone. You will gather data that's going to inform your plan to help you move out and step forward into the dream you seek.

Why is an Informational Interview Important?

An informational interview is important because as you have identified where you want to go, what you want to do, and you recognize the strengths and functional areas you naturally excel in given your matched desire with your matched strength. With the informational interview, you're now going to be on a journey to research where you can integrate those strengths into a career path or plan that's going to be right for you.

An information interview is a conversation with someone in the industry or the area of business or life you want to ask questions about to gather information that will serve to help you in your journey. You're going to conduct an interview. You're going to ask questions of that individual simply to gain information or insight into their perspective about the career, the industry or the role they play in the environment that you are hopeful to work one day. And when you do that, it's going to give you the information necessary to help you come into that environment with answered questions instead of unanswered questions. It will ultimately set you up to be more successful than someone who comes in blind.

Setting Up the Informational Interview

There are two ways you can establish an informational interview. First, you can make cold calls. Consider the company, industry or environment you think you might want to work in and reach out. Look online, find the phone number or a way to make contact and say, "Hey, this is who I am. This is what I'm looking to do. Is there someone in the company I could speak with regarding X position?" They'll likely refer you to a recruiter in the organization, and you can seek that person out.

LinkedIn is another way to do some cold calling if you will. Go online, look at the company profile, perform a LinkedIn search and look for anyone with whom you might already be connected. But if you don't have any connections, you can still reach out through LinkedIn by sending a professional message along the lines of, "This is who I am. This is what I want to do. This is how I came to reach out to you." This is not to say you SPAM anyone; rather, you take a targeted and intentional approach based on the preparation work you completed before taking this step in the process.

While cold calling focuses on connecting with those you don't know, the second type of outreach is a warm lead. The warm lead is about leveraging your network to see who you know in the company or organization that can get you connected to someone that you could then sit down with and ask your questions.

Sticking with our LinkedIn example, you can see who you're connected with on there that either already works at the organization or maybe has a second or third connection that will show up in the profile that you could extend reach. Instead of you making the direct contact, you can reach out to your warm connection and say, "Hey, can you connect me to Nathaniel, Josiah or Sydni? I see they work at this company. I want to do an informational interview related to their particular position or their particular industry."

Once you establish connectivity, begin to form the relationship by reaching out, introducing yourself, explaining your purpose and requesting the meeting. It can be a virtual meeting where you have a phone conversation, or you can do a video. You could also do an in-person or face-to-face meeting. I recommend in-person meetings, if possible, so you have an opportunity to observe the culture and environment within an organization. What might it be like to work in that environment? What is the demeanor of the people? What type of atmosphere exists? Does the culture match the presentation in the organization's online presence? And if you can't do that, the second-best option is to do a video call and the third option to conduct the informational interview via phone call.

Identify who you will interview and why

You should interview someone who is doing the work or is in the position you desire that aligns to your dream or vision for your career and life. The entity where they work should resemble the culture and environment that aligns to your *why*. You want to interview one person or a group of people. You might also consider researching similar work across several industries.

Let's say you want to be an instructional designer. You might reach out to someone like me via LinkedIn, or follow me on social media, and send me a message. In your message, you will outline who you are, why you want to connect and make your request. Be mindful that the response time is not predicated on your schedule, but theirs. Thus, it is good to have more than one individual with whom you wish to connect to maintain momentum and maximize your investment toward your future endeavor. No matter the response time, you will likely receive a response and know if time will be scheduled or if you've been referred to another member of the team. Follow the process as outlined to schedule the time and be sure to honor that commitment.

Continuing our instructional designer example, let's say I respond. I would send you my link to find a time that works best for you on my calendar. We connect and have a conversation about why you want to be an instructional designer, what my experience has been in that particular field, what I like and don't like about it. You might also ask additional questions specific to your niche interest to help inform the direction and decision you desire.

You want to be very specific and targeted, with those you meet because if you're just haphazardly selecting someone to meet with, you're not necessarily going to get the benefit from doing the informational interview, which means you're not going to know what you need to know. You might not be able to fill any gaps in your knowledge about what skills or knowledge you need to have that would allow you to be successful or be able to identify what skills or knowledge are transferrable from what you currently do into the environment you desire to enter. Be intentional with your questions to enable you to close any knowledge or skill-gap concerns regarding how your current job can translate into the desired career you seek.

Ask questions

Simon Sinek wrote a book entitled, *Start With Why.* It's one of the books I was exposed to that changed the questions I propose and the recommendations I make when working with clients. And so number one, start with why. Ask the individual you're meeting with why they chose this career field. What was it about this industry they found appealing or what value was added to their life? Ask them about the community and culture. Is it highly political? Community focused? Collaborative? I would also ask questions about the strategy. How do you do things? How are things done in this industry? How are things done in this business? How do you structure your day? What does a typical day in the life of someone in this role resemble? You might ask about career trajectory or promotional opportunities for someone in this industry. Is this a skill that can transfer to you doing your own thing some day? What has been their experience with vendors in this field? How successfully do they think they would be if they stepped out of a corporate environment maybe into their own business or maybe even working for a different type of business or industry? What attracted them to the industry? What skills are transferable to other areas? What might their next career move be given their current position?

What is their *why?* And why do they continue to work in that particular environment? What is it about it that keeps them there?

This list is not exhaustive but serves as a guide to get you started with asking questions. These can be questions you ask not only for an informational interview but for any career opportunity or a venture you're seeking to step into in the future.

Job Shadow Follow Up

Another method of capturing information is by engaging in a job-shadowing opportunity. Job shadowing is as *an educational program where college students or other adults can learn about a particular occupation or profession to see if it might be suitable for them* (http://www.businessdictionary. com/definition/job-shadowing.html). In other words, a job allows you to ask for an opportunity to come on site and sit with an individual to observe and engage in a day in the life for the role you're seeking. That's going into their environment, attending meetings with them, engaging in conversations and asking them questions while they work.

You will physically sit, where possible, with the person in their space, capturing answers to your questions and observing what's happening around you. You are also making a note of the kinds of questions they're getting asked. What kind of meetings do they participate in or attend? What are they doing in those meetings? What's their contribution to that environment?

By engaging in a job-shadowing opportunity, you are privileged to get a fly-on-the-wall view of the career you are planning to transition into. The insights and perspectives gained from this vantage point will allow you to better formulate your plan how to get there and address the skill gaps you may have identified as a result of this experience.

Identify your skill gaps

Once you've completed your informational interview and a job shadow either with the person you interviewed initially or with someone else on their team, you're equipped with the data to begin formulating your functional fulfillment transition plan. You are now able to reflect on the skills previously identified and your 360 views of who you are and what you bring to the table to empower your decision to change. Let's say, for example, that you observed the woman or man you shadowed consistently making pivot tables throughout their day. You recognize that your skillset does not include knowledge on how to do a pivot table in Microsoft Excel. This is a skill gap that could keep you from attaining your career goal. Take the time to research ways to acquire the skill, either internally or external to your organization. While we only highlight one skill gap here, you may recognize more than one that can lead to greater specificity in your overall development plan.

While you're in the environment, make a note of where you have skill gaps, what you observed that you liked, tools or systems you don't know how to use, or may require a refresh given lack of use of the tool in your daily life. Whatever the gap, you now need to go and make sure you have an opportunity to learn and relearn or be immersed in an environment that will help you to learn how to do a pivot table again so you are equipped to do one should you choose to pursue an opportunity in this environment.

When you've done your informational interview discussion, asked the questions, completed a job shadow, hopefully you've identified where your opportunities or gaps exist and ways to close them. Give yourself no more than 6-9 months to resolve any gaps or areas for concern so you can achieve what you ultimately want to do with your life and aligns with the goals you set for yourself.

4

Determine Your Next Right Step

"Instead of looking at the past, I put myself ahead twenty years and try to look at what I need to do now in order to get there then."

—DIANA ROSS

THIS CHAPTER IS ALL ABOUT CREATING AN ACTION PLAN THAT'S going to help you move and make the transition you desire into your dream career within the next 6-12 months. and if perchance you don't reach that dream, you need to assess your goal. look at your *why.* review your *why* and eliminate any distractions. invest in learning and making sure your skills align with the dream career you've set out to attain.

The action plan is going to help you choose the next right action step to enable you to be successful. Your success with your action plan is predicated upon what you have defined as the goal or desired outcome on this journey. Important to note is that this plan must have an accountability timeline and framework. This isn't a willy-nilly moment during which you arbitrarily select a few targets and hope, wish and pray results manifest. We believe in clarity and defined expectations as you prepare for the transition. We will not *fail to plan nor plan to fail* as espoused by Benjamin Franklin.

Get clear on what you need to do

Where do you need clarity? Most of us don't know where we need clarity nor do we plan because we don't exactly know what we want to do. We're not clear about the direction we wish to take. To gain clarity, review what you value in your life. What is important to you when you think about the next action or right step in your life? What are your life's priorities?

For me, at age 40, my plans and priorities include getting out of debt, stepping fully into what I love to do and taking care of my growing family. In my 30s, I was all about growing my corporate career and starting my family. In my 20s, I was focused on finishing my education and acquiring skills that would lead to the achievement of personal goals that included getting a doctoral degree by age 30 (I was 34), buying my first home as a single woman (achieved), attaining my bachelor's degree in four years (achieved). Becoming CEO of a Fortune 500 company was also on the list and has yet to be achieved, and I am not sure I want that responsibility today as much as I did when I was younger. Our plans evolve and change as we evolve and change.

What about you? At one stage in your 20s, you might have said that your priorities were finishing school and finding the right trade or career. Or in your 30s, the priority might your family and raising your children. Perhaps it's traveling the world, traveling to all 50 states or climbing Kilimanjaro. In your 40s, the priority might be looking at plans to prepare for retirement financially or another life transition. Whatever the goal for the stage of life you're in, prepare to make the transition.

Getting clear on what you need to do is all about looking at what you value and what your priorities are in life. And then putting those in order of importance so you can look at what you desire to do in a career and how you're going to leverage that career or increase in your life. Finally, ensure that it matches up with the priorities you have established in your journey.

Create a plan that marries your values and priorities and requires you to step out and do what you want to do in YOUR life. Let's take a look at a few ways to successfully achieve your desired outcome.

You Must Have Focus

What do I mean by focus? I lacked focus, and it resulted in a great struggle. I like to get my hands in a lot of things. I use the phrase, "I'm a jack of all trades and a master of none." That can work for some people but not everyone. And I've seen when there are too many different areas trying to get your attention; they can become distractions from you being able to go forward in the thing you should be doing.

Focus is all about eliminating distractions and zeroing in on will help you achieve your goals. So how can you do that? If you're like many, your time is inundated with the digital platform – checking email, using social media and carrying your phone. We're always plugged in, so to speak. In this step, the recommendation eliminates the dopamine-infused buzz that emanates from electronic devices and disrupts thought patterns and distractions from the pursuit of our respective why to engage in the sphere of information over-load. I'm not saying to stop using technology; I am recommending that we are more intentional to leverage technology to aid in our ability to focus and build out our most important next right step along the journey.

Instead of handwriting your notes or capturing your thoughts on paper, you might consider using a voice-activated recording device or dictaphone. Sure, most smartphones have this technology, but we both know that those buzzes may get the best of you, and the goal here is to get focused, not distracted. Let's say you are disciplined enough to turn off notifications on your phone and maintain focused attention, then that is the best option to keep this process on the low-investment end. If you're not certain of your capability to focus, then go old school technology and take out a blank piece of paper. I tend to default to the handwriting method as I can get into a thought flow and not be interrupted with an email or a phone ding. I can also turn off my phone or leave it on silent with an alarm to incite my focus for 15 minutes to 1 hour each day. Be intentional and schedule some time to practice thinking into your why and what you want to do. Start small, with no more than a five-minute focus. Write down the question or thought you wish to process, start your timer and write or speak aloud whatever thoughts come to mind about your subject.

Let's make it easier for you to get started. The first focus exercise is a handwriting exercise. Take out paper and a writing utensil, use a stopwatch or notification-free phone clock timer set to 1 minute. Write your name in the center of a piece of paper. Start the timer and begin to write the thoughts that come to mind about you. No matter the thought, the goal is to keep writing during the minute, even if the word or thought begins to repeat itself – DON'T STOP WRITING until the timer goes off. Consider words that describe your calling, purpose or your function that describe who you are and who you believe you were created to be from the beginning of your time on the earth. Once you've completed this step, I want you to take those words and craft a singular sentence that says, "This is who I am" using only the words or phrases written during the exercise. What was your result?

The exercise described can be used for any area of your life that requires focus. If you want to focus on making the career transition in the next 6-12 months, then the singular question you place at the forefront of your mind should be, "What is it going to take for me to get to the career or dream I want to be in within the next 6-12 months? Hold that intent in your mind, and then give yourself 1 minute (gradually work up to 5 minutes) to zero in on the answer. Write everything down that comes to mind during that time, and then take that and create a statement or a sentence. When you create that sentence, it's going to become part of the action plan that will help you to take action steps to propel you forward.

Invest in Learning

I am a lifelong learner, and I believe everyone should be learning constantly. Your car can become a learning laboratory, meaning you can listen to audio books while you're driving instead of the radio or your playlist. You may even opt to leverage commute time as an opportunity to get focused and tap the recorder as you head out stating your question and the thoughts that come to mind as they relate to the answer. Just so we're clear, I'm not opposed to music, in fact, I love music, but when in this transition phase, the investment of time is leveraged as much as possible to attaining the goal. Given my extensive commutes to get my little ones to and from their destinations, I have a minimum of 15–20 minutes each way to process thoughts and questions should I choose. So think about your commute and leverage your transportation as your learning laboratory.

Everywhere you go, there can be time invested in closing the knowledge or skill gaps previously identified to prepare you for the next right step. This could be reading or listening to a book or notating or selecting articles for review. Even as you scroll social media, you should be looking for information to help you acquire knowledge base or skills.

You may also have to consider investing resources which may include money to take a class or two or to attend a workshop on how to write your resume, or how to negotiate your salary, for example. You might decide to pursue an educational certificate or take the required certification program to ensure your readiness for the next life level for you. Regardless of choice to be made, you should identify the actionable steps to get where you want to go and make it part of your functional fulfillment plan.

Investing in learning is the process designed to help you to close the gap you've identified to help you make the next right step as you move forward with purposeful action planning. The expected outcome of your actions is that you can move into the career you desire and ultimately fulfill and align your values and priorities. Whether it's investing time in reading a book, investing time in researching and reviewing articles, investing time in talking with mentors or sponsors or taking class, there has to be action and time set aside. It's time to invest in Y.O.U. (your own unveiling)!

Update Your Resume

Now you know what you want to do, and you have your values and priorities defined, you've addressed the skill gaps with intentional learning investment, it's time to update your resume. Your resume will now serve as a reflection of the research, time and investment you've made to acquire and be able to articulate the direction you wish to go.

Let's take out the piece of paper every company typically requires, your resume (or curriculum vitae if you're in the education industry). Prepare to update the document to reflect the skills you bring to the table, highlighting your strengths. You can do a functional, chronological or combination resume. The combination resume is a functional and chronological resume that highlights the skills and chronology of your experience and work history. The resume should be designed to highlight your strengths, showcase your experience and provide information on the results obtained from your work production. Experience includes all experience – volunteering, work experience, community or board service. It may also include a reference to your hobbies (where relevant), interests you learned about when you took the personality assessment, etc.

Have you ever used the STAR method as a response strategy when interviewing? STAR stands for **S**ituation, **T**ask, **A**ction, **R**esults. When interviewing, you often will describe the **situation or task** that required your involvement. Next, you will highlight the **action** you took to address the situation or task as presented. Then, you will share the **results** of the action you took to meet the desired outcome or goal. When engaging in a behavioral interview environment, the STAR method will help provide the specificity needed to answer the interview questions succinctly.

As you consider your resume, it should serve as a reminder during the interview process of who you are, your strengths, results achieved and career accomplishments to date. Your resume should always focus on the **action** you took in your organization for a particular task, and the **results** attained from your action. The resume is not the time to be modest or humble, but instead to be bold and courageous as you state what you did, how you accomplished it and the output that was yielded.

The resume serves as the gateway to interview opportunities. In other words, if you are not getting access to opportunity in the dream career path, consider why that might be happening. Nine times out of ten, it is a direct result and reflection of your resume. Thus the importance of doing your homework and research BEFORE you consider going elsewhere so you can focus and highlight your strengths and recognize where your gaps were, and how you can overcome the gaps to achieve your desired outcome. You're now ready to articulate your actions and show how you've already demonstrated success in the skills needed for future opportunities.

If your plan doesn't work, what will you do?

William Edward Hickson said "If at first, you don't succeed, try, try again!" He was right! If out of the gate, you do all I've outlined in this manuscript and the transition does not go as planned, DO NOT QUIT! You must remember your why and then D.E.C.I.D.E. how you're going to move forward. The process WORKS if you WORK it!

I am a big proponent of contingency plans. So let's say you did all the work. You identified your values. You've got your priorities. You eliminated distractions and zeroed in on what was going to help to create a focus for you. You've invested in learning from others and identified your gaps. You've updated your resume, and you go after the career you want and it doesn't come to pass. Now WHAT?

A couple of things could be the root cause. It may be the plan you have to leave your corporate job in the next 12 months and go into business full-time needed more time. Let's say your goal was to have the equivalent of one year's salary in the bank. Well, let's say you have $50,000, but your current annual salary is $100,000. As we recommend having at least one year's salary available, maybe more, if you're going into business full-time, then you're not quite ready. Ask yourself if your plan is working. Could you and your family live off $50,000? What if the efforts you expend to generate leads and business yield ZERO results, what would you do? The reality is your plan is working but did not yield in the timeframe you desired. Now ask yourself what actions or activities within the current plan didn't get to the $100,000 that you needed to be able to walk away free and clear at the one-year mark.

What will you do? Well, this is your back-up, or contingency, plan. How are you going to close the $50,000 gap? In this example, what steps are you going to take to close the gap? Are you going to give yourself another six months? Are you going to work a part-time job that will close an identified skill gap *and* help generate income? Will you start a gig leveraging your strengths, (talk to your ethics & compliance team if currently working for an employer)? No matter the response, this is another point of decision that will determine how you plan to move forward.

Another reason to consider is your living and lifestyle choices. Perhaps you're still living in a way that maintains a more lavish lifestyle that could not be sustained without modification. You might consider making some adjustments – downsizing, decreasing your amenities, not eating out or getting manicures and pedicures, etc. The sole purpose and goal here are to look at life differently for a season to empower you to move forward toward the transition you desire.

So really if the plan doesn't work, this is all about looking at why didn't the plan work? And what are you going to do? What are going to be your next steps to bring you on course? This is where your accountability team comes in to serve as advisors to you as you are in the valley of decision. Your support network, your tribe, is there to help you get to the goal so you can reach the vision that you've established for yourself and shared with those around you. There should be some tough love inquiries as to why you have not yet completed the task before you, and there should be encouragement and support to help you move forward.

Determine how to turn what you love into a profitable opportunity

Once you've identified what you love to do, you want to think about how you can begin doing it. If you're already working in a job that perhaps you don't like or even one you hate, but it is paying the bills, keep working in that job. While working in that job, begin to look at ways you can take what you've learned in the course of your journey toward the career you want and begin to look at how you can make money.

One way might be to go on social media, specifically Facebook, and offer a four-week class on how to do X, where the X is whatever you love to do, or a strength that can be used to begin making money. This might resemble a one-day workshop or a half-day workshop. The idea here is to begin to look at those strengths, those things you love to do and identify ways you can create an opportunity to make money.

A few suggestions to join the gig economy is to leverage social media, have a garage sale, host a webinar, or use an online platform to create a course or series of courses to generate income. Use what you have in your hands to build the life and legacy that yields your desired lifestyle. Whatever you decide, don't wait – do it now! The action your take at this stage also continues the journey to identify and close any skill gaps.

In March 2019, I was privileged to attend an event with Dr. Tom Anderson during which he discussed principles and ways to build wealth. He consistently said, "You buy low and sell high." As the discussion continued, he shared an example of how our mindset impacts our ability to create profitability in our lives. The example was, "If I were to give you $10 and I said to you, you have 30 days to turn that $10 into $20, what would you do?" The idea here is to take the concept of turning $10 to $20 using solely those areas you've identified as strengths or looking at what you love to do to create income now before your plan has fully matured. Here's what I love to do. Here's what brings me joy and fulfillment. And pretend that I'm going to give you $10 to make it $20 in the next 30 days. So, how are you going to get that $20?

5

Invest in Yourself

"I got my start by giving myself a start."
—MADAME CJ WALKER

NO ONE IS GOING TO GIVE YOU WHAT YOU WERE DESIGNED and crafted to unveil or unearth from the inside of yourself. The work to be done requires you to "dig for gold" from within so you can shine bright on the exterior. I've been told that I'm very self-aware. One of the encounters I recall was following an interview for an opportunity.

During this particular interview, I was nine weeks pregnant and hosting the conversation with a peppermint tucked in the side of my jaw to keep nausea at bay during the conversation. I answered each question truthfully and honestly. After the formal discussion, the interviewer stated: "You're very self-aware." I paused and said thank you, and it stuck. Here's why: The interviewer noticed the level of clarity about myself, who I was at that time and my future goals. I could articulate my strengths and express my gaps clearly, which enabled me to share candidly what I expected to gain from the role and what I would bring to the team should I be their top candidate.

So what does that mean for you? It means that you have to be prepared to state your goals, highlight your strengths, recognize your gaps and have an action plan to showcase your value within the first 90 days in the role should you be given the opportunity. You have to become more self-aware, which will translate into authenticity and transparency between you and those you choose to serve. Invest the time to grow and develop beyond where you are so that you can more immediately articulate how you add value.

Invest in you – strengthen your strengths and demonstrate your uniqueness so you become the person that is full of life, the vigor that can then help you to move toward the dream you set out to achieve. And it includes personal development as well as the professional development aspect, which requires you to have a holistic approach to how you're going to move your life forward.

Personal Growth and Development

Develop yourself holistically. To do so requires the development of skills, an increase in knowledge and an expansion on your belief about your ability to complete a task or accomplish a set goal. It requires a commitment to change from what is known and familiar to enable growth beyond your current situation.

Personal development also includes the inner work necessary to gain mental clarity. It's what allows us to look at the motive behind our plans. It requires care and thoughtful consideration, and reinforces our position and standards on why we do what we do. Personal growth also necessitates a need to be physically healthy. We cannot carry out the vision or live out our why if we are bedridden, sick or shut-in. No one knows our bodies better than we do, and it is okay to learn and grow to achieve optimal health in the pursuit of what you love. Ultimately, growth includes the journey to educate yourself in an area you have a gap or a lack of knowledge. As we've looked at what we want to do, we recognize that we might have a strength in one area and there might be gaps in other areas that also need to be strengthened. We don't want to be lopsided in our development approach where only one part of us is strong. That can create an internal imbalance that we then have to spend more time trying to uncover and recover.

Personal development and growth require a holistic approach to self, that self-awareness of mind, spirit, soul, body, time, money and relationships. Are you managing your time effectively? Is there an intelligent, emotional aspect to things that need to be looked at and reviewed? Are your relationships healthy? Are you in a perpetual cycle of emotional reactions? Where and when are you engaging the inner part of who you are? Are you on an assignment exchanging time for money or receiving money for the value you add where you serve? Are you living the life you desire and intended? Why or why not? The answers to these questions takes us back to our "why" and helps us to define the holistic approach to growth.

Find A Coach

A coach can help you look at blind spots you might have that keep you from being whole. And it's not just about those blinders. In the words of Christian Simpson, a coach helps you to "make the unconscious conscious." Said differently, a coach should be helping you to get uncomfortable by asking questions to help you think into yourself, your perceptions and ideals. Those are those areas in our life that perhaps we don't recognize that we are not whole, or where we might have blinders on that keep us from being able to make progress. We often think we are, but we are not.

A coach is not going to give you answers or advice. They are going to help you to think into yourself and about where you might actually have those blinders, and help you get the clarity necessary for you to be able to step forward into the things you say are your goals, your dreams and your vision.

Hiring a coach is an extremely important investment to make because it's going to help you reveal the unconscious part of you. Once you have that awareness, you're now able to take action on how you're going to move it forward. You might find something in you that's a good thing you need to keep. Or you might find there's a blind spot or an area that needs further development.

Your coach, in many cases, is not a licensed counselor or therapist; therefore, your coach might recommend you hire a professional therapist. This is a must to help you dig deeper into things that can lead to overall mental and emotional health. I'm all for that because mental health is important.

A coach is not a counselor, and a coach is not your mentor or your advisor. They are a coach. Think about a coach on a team. They're not playing the sport. What they're doing is guiding individuals on the team to operate and function in their place of strength to enable participation within a team and life. There are practices, skill building, accountability and a relationship. There are times to support and times to bring correction for direction. The coach always knows the time, and in most successful teams, there is an established mutual trust.

Those who have helped me in my life are coaches. They helped me get out of my way and gain the clarity I sought, or guided me in the direction I already knew I wanted to go. They brought awareness to the unconscious mindsets that were impacting my life, my career and my family. A coach is going to help you get out of your way by bringing you to a place of awareness and consciousness that will then allow you to move forward without excuse. They also become a member of your support team and hold you accountable for your life and the things you set out to accomplish.

So I'm absolutely on board with finding and hiring a coach. I think everybody needs a coach. Every coach needs a coach, and every person should have a coach to help them see what they can't see within themselves and discover ways to unveil who they were meant to become.

Take Care of Your Health

One of the things I found when I stepped away from Corporate America into entrepreneurship was that I spent 90% of my time at work despite my best efforts. I had no balance. Yes, I had a spouse, children at home, a full-time job and I engaged in other outside activities, but the balance did not exist, and my health was beginning to show it.

I had tension headaches, muscle cramping, knots in my shoulder, neck and shoulder pain where I would constantly feel like I was lifting my shoulders. All resulting from stress and strain of engaging in only one true activity – work. I knew it had become a problem when I went into pre-term labor at 28 weeks with my second child. I nearly miscarried at the beginning of the pregnancy as I had taken on a highly visible and transformational work initiative met with resistance from those who wanted the job but did not receive it. Then not even two months later, I was back in the emergency room threatening to miscarry again, not realizing I had been in labor for nearly 24 hours (I previously had a c-section). So, there I was in pain trying to finish the presentation for the annual meeting, in labor, not recognizing how much pressure, stress and strain I had put on myself and my little one. I had to decide to change and with the stern message from my support system, I willingly adapted my lifestyle and approach, opened the communication lines with my new leader and carried him to term safely. At the pinning of this chapter, he will be four in three days.

Your situation may not be as dire as mine. Do you know someone in your circle with health issues resulting from a dead-beat job? Taking care of yourself first is important. You should not attempt to take care of others without putting yourself at the top of the list, especially if you're working in an environment you do not enjoy nor can find meaning or purpose within. Maintaining health requires commitment and discipline. Most of us do not have discipline in our approach to how we live our lives, and that affects every aspect of our health. It also affects the way we work and how we show up at work. As was the situation for me, I didn't know who I was nor what I wanted and found that my identity was wrapped up in the job I did. I was unhealthy not just physically, but emotionally and mentally. The source of who I was became the thing I was doing.

When the time came, a demotion opportunity presented itself which meant a title change; I didn't know what to do even though I wanted and asked for the change. I found myself in a mind battle about who I was further hindering my health.

Thoughts and intentions were met with fear and began to burrow into the inner places, causing me for a moment to believe that I was not worthy, that I was rejected, that I brought this on myself. More than anything, I felt like a failure, was disappointed in myself for "underperforming" and became overly critical of all I had accomplished. I didn't care about winning the Global Talent Champion award nor the fact that the project many before me had tried to deliver had succeeded on my watch despite myriad changes. My mental health caused fear and anxiety which led to more health issues. I believed I had no control and nearly lost it all because of it.

I want you to know how important it is to become healthy in the pursuit of what you love. Learn to take care of yourself now and evaluate what's important to you mentally, spiritually and physically. Get disciplined in those areas so you can move forward, and so you can be ready to approach your life the way you want to approach it, the way that's going to be healthiest for you and for those around you, and that will benefit you more than anything else I say in this book.

Stay Disciplined

Find a place, a mentor, a speaker, a trainer, or a video series you can model or pattern after that offers a consistent structure, and do it. This is discipline. Doing so will allow you to be steady in your approach to life and living.

Here's an example. "Why is it important to get up and make your bed every day?" Because it creates a sense of purpose, an action that moves you forward in the day. It can set the tone for what you set out to accomplish. Each day it's your choice, you can remember why it's important, then decide on what action you will take. Consider your current daily actions: You wake up, shower or bathe (I hope), get dressed, eat breakfast or drink your beverage of choice, get in the vehicle, drive to the office, work, eat, get in the car, drive home, have dinner and prepare to wake up and do it again tomorrow. Right? It's standardized and somewhat routine. Embedded within it is the discipline it takes to accomplish those respective activities.

When you step into your dream or the career you love, that routine won't necessarily be there in the manner described.

It may be that you modify and adjust how, when and where you show up. It may not feel fluid. It may feel uncomfortable. You might discover new ways to engage in activities that result in a less standardized approach. The result may be a happier, healthier version of your self. Without discipline, it's possible to fall back into unhealthy habits. By having discipline and committing to it, you're going to have consistency and routine. Would life be more enjoyable if instead of going to the office, you travel to the coffee shop, go to a networking meeting, meet with a mentor, conduct some more informational interviews meet with someone to update your resume? Whatever it is, choose to maintain that continuity and the discipline in your routine so you can maintain your overall health.

Skillset Development

Skillset development goes back to what we talked about in the previous chapter regarding investing in learning. I didn't want you initially to focus on the skill development specifically; rather, I encouraged you to take a holistic approach that could be focused and intentional. Let's talk about your specific skills and how you can better them.

When I coach my clients, part of the objective is to focus on strengthening strengths and strengthening the growth areas or opportunities. Everything is going to be strengthened here in the skillset development phase. Feedback is data. It provides you with information that can be analyzed and interpreted and used to create insights, inferences and recommendations for improvement. Where can you find this data? One area you can always revisit is your performance review or annual evaluation. Review the comments, whether or not you agreed with them, examine what was said and how it was stated. Create questions to follow up on and identify ways you can begin to showcase or demonstrate what was presented.

For example, if someone said you don't build relationships well, you might not agree because perhaps you build relationships differently than they do. Maybe there was a personality conflict with someone who made a complaint, and there was only one data point your manager received and no further research was done. As a colleague said, one data point does not a trend make. So ask for three to five examples of where the behavior was demonstrated. Even if there is only one example provided, you can't ignore that piece of. What you might have to do is ask, "What can I do differently? How can I improve in that particular area around building relationships? If we're in meetings together, will you provide me immediate feedback on what you observed regarding how I chose to build relationships in that meeting?" What was in the feedback that was specific about your relationship building that needs further development? Was it your communication in relationships? Was it how you approach meetings? Or was it your email communication?

Skills such as how to write an email or how to build your emotional intelligence skills can yield further development with the right training environment. We can look at developing those skills by investing in classes, coaching or other creative ways that provide exposure to skill-build the identified area of growth.

The more you invest in ways to identify your skill gaps, the better the investment you can make to close the information gap through learning and development activities that yield desired results from experience, exposure or education.

Find Conferences

You should be attending conferences related to your current or desired industry. Every industry has professional associations or not-for-profit organizations where membership opportunities avail. Likely, there's a conference offered annually or semi-annually you should be attending.

If you're an engineer, there's the National Society for Black Engineers, or NSBE. If you're a learning and development professional, there's the Association for Training and Development (ATD). If you're a Paparazzi consultant or any direct-sales organization or offer sales and marketing funnels using tools like ClickFunnels, there's typically an annual conference where strategy is shared, new technologies are demonstrated and trends are introduced. There are also workshops or training that can help to further advance your knowledge or skill in a specific area, typically taught by those who wrote the content or have the experience to share with the group.

Conferences tend to highlight and focus on the skills, knowledge or abilities that are trending in the industry. Your role is to look at the skills you identified previously and identify the workshops or activities that can serve to be enhanced or strengthened given your attendance. Focus on no more than three skills you want to strengthen and three areas of growth you want to focus on for the next six to nine months.

6

Build Your Network Before You Need It

*"One important key to success is self-confidence.
An important key to self-confidence is preparation."*

—ARTHUR ASHE

THIS CHAPTER IS EXTREMELY IMPORTANT BECAUSE IT'S ALL about leveraging your influence and looking at how that influence can be utilized to help you achieve something great. People may have never heard your name or ever met you. You've never done anything for them, so they don't know you. They've never followed you on social media. You've got to begin to build that network now. It was a vital, hard lesson for me.

Let's talk about my experience in identifying how to write a book. I wouldn't have written this book without my network, without leveraging the relationships and influences that were formed before this vision came into manifestation. I began the book-writing journey with the notion that I would write a collaboration book. I reached out to individuals within my network fully confident there would be no hesitation and I would easily get six individuals to partner with me. Who doesn't want to write a book, right? I failed very quickly and recognized that I didn't have as great as an influence or network as I thought I did. In the previous organization where I worked, I had amassed a great network inside of the company, connecting with people all over the world. When I left, I had no network outside of that company because I had let it all go. I don't want you to let go of the network you have, either inside or outside your organization. Be intentional about building relationships and learn ways to connect with people that extend beyond your work environment.

Build the network before you ever need it and establish yourself as an influencer, as a person who gets things done and as someone who is going to add value to people no matter what without needing them in return. And when you are ready to present an offer or opportunity, you'll be ready to leverage the relationship because you built the relationship first.

Say it with me, "Every day, in every way, I build relationships well." I want you every day, in every way, to build relationships well before you even need them so you can influence first without needing them for your success. When you are ready, people will be ready to support you because they'll know you. They'll like you, and they'll trust you.

Identify Your Support Structure - Your Transformation T.R.I.B.E.

This is the group of people that are going to be there to help you process the decisions, to help you finalize where you want to go and who will be there no matter the cost.

They are your trustworthy, real, integral, brilliant, encouragers who serve as your support structure in the journey toward life transformation. Think about customer service. They're the support structure for large companies. They're there to answer the questions and help process the way to get something accomplished. That's support structure. You need that. You need a personal support structure or transformation T.R.I.B.E. in your life. And they're there to help you make decisions, process your decisions, answer questions and ask the questions that might cause discomfort or challenge your BS (Bogus Stories). Why are you thinking that way? Why do you feel like you can't do this? Why are you so nervous about this opportunity or stepping out into this role, stepping out to do your own business? They are there to help with the clarity, your vision and making sure it stays before your eyes.

Your T.R.I.B.E. is important in that they are part of your transformation and accountability team. They're going to be there to help you move forward and get to the place in the life of success you desire to achieve. If you're surrounded by people individuals who aren't trustworthy, real, integral, brilliant in their own right or encouraging –get a new T.R.I.B.E.!

Tell Your Peers

Your peers are individuals in your circle of influence. Perhaps they've been there when you worked in an environment you hated. They may have been your trusted advisor. They may also be individuals you're spiritually connected to on one level or another. They may be individuals who share your skillsets, solo comrades in the journey of entrepreneurship or in the journey of your corporate venture or whatever you seek to do.

They are on the same level, or in the same space, in most instances, that you find yourself. But sometimes they also have a higher view. They might also have lived a life beyond where you are and can bring a unique perspective to the table, but they still know you well enough to help you process whatever you desire to move forward into. These individuals are part of your network. They're connected. They're influencers. And they're available to bring you back to light and life after you share your deepest, darkest moments. They might let you go there for a moment, but they're going to help you come back to life, and then they're going to resuscitate you. They're your emergency team. They're going to breathe life back into you, kick you in the butt, get you back out there and say, "No, this is how we're going to do this. This is what you need to do." They're going to help to move you forward.

I know, this is not the standard definition that your peer is someone who shares the same job title or position with you. Nor is it someone who shares the same pay grade level. I refer to those individuals, with whom no relationship exists, as colleagues or associates because there is an association that constitutes being grouped together; however, the lack of relationship changes the level of engagement with this group versus the peer as described.

Peers value and recognize what you bring to the team, project or environment. They don't dismiss or discount getting to know you, because their only need for you is the task at hand. Peers are part of the network you need. They understand what it's going to take for you to achieve what you need to achieve spiritually, emotionally and physically. They might be there mentally, but they know your business. They know your industry. They know what concerns you.

And most importantly, they know you, and they're going to help you. They're going to resuscitate you when needed. Share the vision with your peers so they can celebrate you as you journey onward.

Leverage Social Media

Technology has enabled us to connect whenever we want or choose to engage in communication. Social media is a way that allows us to connect with others more quickly. And it gives us greater visibility to others when we connect to them. Thus, it is vital to building your network before you need to because you might post something that gets shared by one of your friends to a friend. The next thing you know, the six degrees of separation is no longer a separation, and your network expanded due to the connection you have with one. When you begin to step out into your dream, into the thing you're seeking, you're going to be able to leverage social media to help you achieve your dreams and goals.

It's extremely important to network inside and outside of your organization. It's something I didn't do very well. I have a lot of followers, but you don't just want a lot of people following you. You want them validating the information you're putting out there. You want them sharing it. You want to know they're influencers, that they're sharing the information, helping to propel it forward. It helps provide social capital validation and makes proposed ideas and concepts, viable concepts and ideas.

Once you've identified the importance for you, you will want to do it. Here's one way I leverage social media and recommend you do it. Go live on a social media platform for 30 days. Someone challenged me to do that. It was very eye-opening. I honestly tried to hide and do it late at night, and I still had people watching and engaging at 11 PM CST. So there's no excuse. You can do it at any time of the day. You can record your videos and upload them. You can use tools to help you post on your social media constantly. You want to post as often as possible, at least 12 to 16 times a day, the last statistic I read. You want to constantly have information related to the dream, related to who you are and who you're becoming out there. It might be a quote. It might be offering a workshop we talked about previously, or some training or a how-to product or an advertisement that you're going to launch a new service. You may have written a book, and you're going to put a statement out there that says, "Hey, I'm excited to announce I'm writing a book." Whatever it is, you're going to leverage social media as a tool to help you build the network to begin to promote your strengths, your expertise in an area and help you become connected to those who can help propel you into your next right step. It may even lead to becoming profitable and allow you to move beyond employment to entrepreneurship if you desire.

Ask for Support

Many people don't like to ask for help. As a result, you might be sitting there thinking, I know how to design the training, and I know how to facilitate the training. What I don't know how to do is market myself. What I don't know how to do is get people to buy my product. You may need some help, and that goes back to the peer group and support structure. Asking for their support in pointing you to resources, people, training or development tools, or just pointing you in the direction of the help you need to go forward. The goal is to get you positioned and pointed where you desire to go.

Here's an example: I connected with someone from one organization that I'm a part of, and she created a private Facebook group. I joined that group. In that group, I met someone who was always talking about writing a book. I sat there thinking that I needed to write one. This thought precipitated action. I reached out through the Facebook Messenger and said, "All right, I think I'm ready. What's it going to take?" She invited me to a webinar. I watched the webinar, which led to me wanting to do a collaboration book. And so I found the resources. No excuses. Find your resources. Find the resources you need to achieve what you desire. I found the resources to make it happen. I embarked upon the journey, and here I am today doing a solo book project instead of a collaboration project as a result.

And so I asked for support because yes, I could have done the book myself. I have all the tools and resources. I know how to publish books. I just needed the accountability. I needed the support structure. I needed someone to tell me, "Hey, this is not good." And I wanted that. And so because I asked for it, I received it. You need accountability and support structure. Everybody does. And you need to ask for it when you're not sure how you're going to get from point A to point B. That support structure is there to help you achieve that goal and move you forward. So don't be afraid to ask. Ask for what you need today.

Consider the phrase, "the world is your oyster," which can serve as an illustration for how we spend our lives – cozy and comfortable. Have you ever considered that the oyster has more than one function? It can be served as food or produce pearls. The multi-faceted nature of an oyster allows it to perform its function consistently and without fail. Why? Because it has no voice and no choice in its function or purpose. You have a voice *and* a choice. Use the voice to ask for what you want or for help when needed, and choose how you will align with others to reach your optimal level of performance.

Go to Networking Events

It's essential to go to networking events because they serve as another way to build and share your expertise. It's part of the process to learn to market yourself. It's part of that personal brand. It's part of sharing your skillset and being able to begin to leverage the skills before you need them. It's learning what's out there in the marketplace.

Networking events are vital to your success as an individual who wants to grow in your career. Your next step in a career might be at the networking event. There might be opportunities available every day for jobs, career opportunities that never get posted because osomeone at a networking event engaged in conversation with another, built a relationship beyond the one-and-done a meeting, learned of the opportunity and were prepared to move forward in the process. They get the job. You may not ever have known it was available. What's the difference? The person was known, liked and had created a level of trust to lead to a conversation where her name was mentioned. How did the person know about her skills? She told them. She took the time to promote and market her skills, knowledge and ability during opportune moments. She wasn't seeking to promote or leave the team; rather, her focus was on building the relationship, which provided the opportunity to share. You can go, be yourself and transparent so people know a little bit about who you are beyond the resume. There's a collaboration, collaborative opportunities there that you might get a chance to work on some projects through that organization or networking event that you might not otherwise have been able to get exposure to in your corporation or on your own.

Networking events are another vital piece of your success. In-person contact is going to be what helps you move beyond the now into the next thing, because there will be people there who can push you.

How do you find networking events? In the organization for which you work. Professional associations or industry associations often have networking events. There's Eventbrite, Meetup, the LinkedIn community, Twitter and Facebook events. You can now put your city and state in there and see all the events happening in your local community.

As a result, you can find opportunities to network. Your local Chamber of Commerce, your community boards and your Church are all avenues at which you can identify networking events to make connections, collaborate with others and create the community that's going to help you to move your dreams forward.

Join organizations

There are ample organizations out there. Perhaps you were a Girl Scout, for example, when you were young. And now you haven't had any connectivity to Girl Scouts because there wasn't a transition from high school into college at the time of your membership. There is today, and there's also an alumni network. You could look at how you can rejoin Girl Scouts at the alumni level. There are fraternities and sororities. There are other non-profits. There are boards. You can serve on a board of directors by volunteering.

Look over charitable organizations such as the American Red Cross, the American Cancer Society or the American Heart Association. They are always looking for volunteers and individuals to become a part of their community.

You can choose to join those organizations, often for little to no cost. There are also homeless shelters, etc. ... I could go through a laundry list of volunteer organizations. There are also opportunities to lead in those organizations, to volunteer and serve. There is an opportunity for you to step into a leadership role that can help you to gain some skillsets beyond what you can gain in any of the other environments we've discussed.

Volunteerism is influencing people. You can learn to influence people in a volunteer environment in which people don't have to report to you or get a paycheck from you; one in which they are simply there because they have chosen to and want to be there. There's no better leadership training ground than a volunteer organization, and I think that is important when you're building your network, because it also helps you to stay grounded in who you are and why you initially set out on this journey that goes well beyond money as the motivator but allows you to look at what motivates you and others beyond.

7

Market Yourself Accordingly

"If I didn't define myself for myself, I would be crunched into other people's fantasies for me and eaten alive."

—AUDRE LORDE

THIS CHAPTER IS REALLY ABOUT YOU AND THE MESSAGE YOU send to others. Who you are is the message. It is the image. It is the brand and the language others will communicate about you. Marketing yourself accordingly, you've done the legwork. If you followed all the steps and recommendations in the book, you are now ready to take your niche and get your riches. Well, I make no promises that you will be rich, but your life will be enriched by how you chose to change and embrace it to become more fulfilling for you. As a result of that, you're ready to share your message with the world. You're ready to be the message you intended for others to see and share that. That's what this chapter is all about.

Reframe Your Brand

Your brand is the image others have of you. More specifically it's not what you do, not the job title or the company that you represent, but you. Who are you? What is your mantra? When they hear your name mentioned, what word or words are automatically associated? That is your brand.

This section is really about reframing that brand. You might not even know your brand. At this point, it's a good time to reflect on all you learned through your interviews and job shadows and other aspects during which you asked questions of others. And as you've been looking at your skill set, what is your brand? Talking with others is going to help you get some of that information; you might also consider developing a brief mini survey that says, "When you hear my name, what comes to mind?"

Earlier I mentioned the 360 assessment. That's going to give you some insight into your brand. And in some cases, you have to decide what you want that brand to be. For example, if you hear the name Oprah Winfrey, what images or words come to mind? I would immediately associate her name and her brand with wealth and giving because in my mind, she's a giver, and she's a wealthy giver. So what image or words come to mind when your name is mentioned? You can shape those word or image associations with your choices and actions.

What would your current leader or boss say about you when your name is mentioned? What would your peers say? What would your family say? What would your friends say? The responses from each group are what constitute your personal brand. For starters, you have to define what you want that personal brand to be. And also, if it doesn't align after you've asked yourself those series of questions, with who you want to be, then it's time to reframe it. Given that you've already identified the job your currently doing isn't perhaps what you want to do, you are ready to choose to step into a career that allows you to leverage what you love and creates a brand that matches. You want your name to be synonymous with the brand you're seeking to create by doing the thing you love.

Get comfortable promoting you

Self-promotion is uncomfortable for most, especially women. As a result, women tend not to want to put themselves out there. She doesn't want to take the risk to say, "Hey, I'm excellent at this," or, "This is what my uniqueness brings to the table." Nothing against women, but we are not necessarily always comfortable with self-promotion. Why? Because we usually tend to be taking care of other people. That said, some men have this issuea, but it's not as pervasive as women. We have to get comfortable with stating to others that at which we excel.

For example, I am a good instructional designer, but I wouldn't nor could I have said that three years ago. Today I can say that confidently and not feel bad or not be removed because other people are better than me. I know what you're thinking, "Why didn't she say she's great at it?" I learned from John C. Maxwell that we can always get better. My level of comfort with promoting myself in that particular skill had to grow and mature as I grew. This will also be true for you. As you grow, what you once believed to be your greatest asset will change. By being able to control how you change, you will control how you show up in every environment.

Continuing the example, I am a good designer (see what I did there?), but having said that I also recognize that I like helping to set up a training and development foundation for organizations. So I don't want to be your instructional designer forever, but I want to be the instructional designer who can come in and help you create the strategy and build the framework that's going to take you forever. Note the difference between my original statement and this latter statement. The more confident you are in who you are and what you love to do, the more it will show up in how you activate yourself, take action and your demonstrate your attitude. Let's call this *actitude*.

It's important to have your strengths identified, know what you want, and set your priorities and values because in that you're going to be able to confidently say, "I am good at this." Take a moment to identify what are you good at and write a statement that says, "Here's what I'm good at," so you can begin to practice saying it over and over again until its fluid and rolls off your tongue in conversation. It becomes part of your elevator pitch and can easily be used to address the question, "Tell me a little bit about yourself." Your response should resemble, "Thank you for asking. Let me share with you what I love to solve for others. I am good at…" Complete the sentence with what you're good at and love to get to do with others as partners.

What Resources Do You Have?

Everything you need is on the inside of you to accomplish your dream and find the fulfilling career you desire. What do I mean by that? Those resources are your mind. What's in your head? What is in your hands? The things you have already begun to do the work for, the resources available to you, the resources you have are at your disposal. And it's not just what's on the inside but your network, the people with whom you are connected. In that first contract, can they help you with promoting you by serving as a sponsor for your next right career move, or promoting your business and sharing with others?

It might be a thing that's starting in your garage. It might be that you love making jewelry and that's wonderful. What do you already have? And what are you already doing? How can you leverage that as a resource to begin to market yourself accordingly and looking at the people you're connected with to help you do that now versus later?

What Resources Do You Need?

First you have to look at what you have available. Once you recognize what you have in your hands identified as skill, knowledge and relationships, acknowledge any gaps with what you have versus what you might need to accomplish.

Consider someone who has great analytical and political skills in the workplace. She is adept at what she does but does not recognize how her strength adds value to the organization. Given her excellence and capability to achieve the desired outcome efficiently, she is overworked. She is presented with an opportunity to offload work, but it doesn't cause changes to occur within the team. Having hired a coach, she is made aware that her greatest way to combat the feeling of the lack of support is to leverage her strength and create a report that highlights the work on her plate. At this stage, she doesn't need many resources. If I know I have a great network and I'm getting 100 hits on my jewelry-making product idea, and people are sharing it, and I'm getting a lot of orders for jewelry making.

Then I know I have a good network. But what do I need? In this particular instance, what I might need is a better system for how I leverage that network because right now, it's word of mouth. Right now, it's emailed. Right now, it's just my customer base. I'm also finding that I'm getting so many orders that I can't keep up with the demand. So the supply is great, or you've got a lot of demand, but you don't have enough supply. Maybe it's time to expand the team. The great work is resultant from engaging in the career you love and leveraging that career and that skill set to create ways to expand your team.

You are also looking at all the variables and what you have access to in order to begin to build the framework that's going to help you to sustain your functional fulfillment plan.

Tips to Marketing Yourself

It's important to market yourself because you can't expect or have the expectation that others will market you.

I saw an example when I worked in a corporate environment in which someone went to act on my behalf and ended up getting the position I desired. And I thought, wow that was interesting. Standing back and observing that experience, I recognized very quickly that I couldn't rely on other people to represent me well. You have to represent yourself. You're your best brand ambassador. And there can be others who are sponsors for you and can speak well on your behalf, and you created a personal brand that when people hear your name, they associate it with the thing you want them to associate, but no one can represent you better than you. You are your best brand ambassador for marketing yourself.

Here are some tips: You've already identified your uniqueness and those things that are your niche area. Step one is to make sure you are recognized for your expertise. Are there ways to do this? Yes. Share your expertise willingly and freely with others, sharing the learned lessons. Writing a book is a great way to market yourself make sure you leverage your networking, always looking at how this helps other people. And not that, but how what you do adds value to others. You are making sure your message is the message you always intended, and sharing that message consistently in every platform available to you on social media, in doing workshops and when you hold an event if you attend an event and you ask a question. If you're in a company and asked to lead a committee, or you're serving on a project team, those tips are ways for you to help to market yourself. You are your best ambassador, and how you interact with and engage other people is going to speak to your brand beyond anything else you could ever do.

Think outside the box (even though I'm a ___, I can still partner with ___)

It's important to think outside the box because a box is limiting. It has four sides. The box in and of itself can only contain or hold that which you put into it. It's important to think outside of the box because perhaps the box itself could be the thing that's going to get you where you need to go. If you step outside of that box, outside of your bubble, outside of your title, outside of your industry, outside of your environment, you might find others who have a similar thought pattern. Or you might find an opportunity for the niche that you created to be leveraged in an environment that's not your current location. It doesn't mean that you throw it away. I believe there are creative ideas and witty inventions in each one of us. Take those ideas, write them down but don't try to fit them within the box of where you currently are in your life. It may not fit in that box; however, when you step outside of what's comfortable and familiar and allow yourself to enter an environment that might be unfamiliar, you might find that that idea, that invention you had actually fit over there versus here where you currently exist.

I was attending a networking event for my business, and one of the ladies I met said she has a yoga studio, and we should partner up. And I was thinking, well I'm a personal and professional development coach. I don't do yoga. But instead of saying what I don't do or what I couldn't do, I had to stop and think outside the box for a moment. How could I? I could leverage the yoga studio to conduct yoga leadership training. Talk about unique. We're going to offer yoga leadership training. And what is that going to look like? She and I had no idea, but we could partner, and we could start brainstorming and thinking of ways we could take what we both bring to the table uniquely and leverage that to create this concept that became a unique niche idea.

You can do the same thing. Even though you're an animator, you can still partner with a training development manager. You can partner with anyone. Take that as an exercise. Think about and say, "Even though I'm an X, I can still partner with Y, and together we'll create a unique thing, Z." That's what's going to help us. Create a niche that will help you to learn to be more marketable because people will see you're limitless in how you approach your business and your strength, and how you leverage that in life and work.

BONUS – Transition to Entrepreneurship

"The progress of the world will call for the best that all of us have to give."

—MARY MCLEOD BETHUNE

I DECIDED TO ADD THIS BONUS CHAPTER BECAUSE IT WAS MY transition. When I became focused on my dreams, while working in corporate America, one of the things I consistently found myself saying is, "One day I'm going to have my own business." Maybe I perceived that was going to be part of my future, and I understood this idea of entrepreneurship and what potential it has for an individual, for the family and for the legacy.

I had a vision beyond myself. We all do, and it may have to be uncovered. We have things that are unique on to us we can leverage to move us closer to the dreams and visions we seek. Entrepreneurship to me is one of the best ways to leverage our skills and unique gift mix. It's going to create great opportunities for success for you, your family and your loved ones.

Starting in business full-time was what I did that felt right to me. And it may be the thing that feels right to you. There are so many companies that have been around for decades that are no longer here because technology is changing the way we do business. Why not go ahead and take a proactive approach in finding your unique gift mix and being prepared so that you can sustain the life that you want to live through becoming your entrepreneur and leveraging your skillset?

Writing a book is one way to begin your business-building journey. Writing a book can lead to speaking engagements or TV appearances, spots on the local news, etc. In one example, there is a company that began building furniture in its garage, and people loved what they built. Soon, their friends and family wanted the furniture, and it grew. It started small, but now they have a retail storefront. And now, the company that was originally limited to local is national. As people have moved out of the area, those people, their friends and loved ones are saying, "Hey, wait a minute. I love this piece. Where did you get it?" It continued to grow. They're hiring more people.

It doesn't matter what your unique gift mix is. It could be a service, whatever you have, this entrepreneurship thing is real, and that's where the money is. Online classes, online opportunities. Amazon is essentially an online business. How much do they own in products? What services do they provide except that they give you a platform with the technology you can leverage to sell services and products? And companies that are their brands are doing that. You might as well get your piece of the pie, but first, you have to do the required work. If you do the work we talked about in the previous chapters, it's going to be a viable option for you to take your unique gift mix and your ideas forward and actually establish your own business apart from working for others, although that might still be something you do for a while.

What is Entrepreneurship?

Entrepreneurship is being organized, managing and taking on all of the risk and responsibility that comes with leading a business that you have created individually or collectively with a group of other people for an exchange of goods and services.

In the United States, it's how this country grew, based upon individuals who had businesses. And we used to live and abide in an apprenticeship world where you got to learn the craft. You didn't go into debt to do that. You spent time learning and studying others and building that up.

Entrepreneurship is just being able to take what you've learned and developed over time and its unique perspective, that unique skill, and putting your unique spin on it to solve a problem. That's what entrepreneurship is all about. It's an answer to an unanswered problem.

As an entrepreneur, I am an answer to a problem. And whatever that problem is, and how it's defined, I'm here to help solve it and resolve it. Whether you're creating an invention that helps you warn someone that they've left their baby in the car or you are a coach who's helping to unveil someone's consciousness, you are here to help solve a problem that was presented to you.

Why is it important?

Entrepreneurship today is important because there are so many companies that have been around for 50, for 60 and 100 years. They're no longer viable. People are losing their jobs left and right. People are being laid off, and there's nothing for them to fall back on.

I don't want to see that happen to anybody. I don't want to see people give their life to an organization and yet the thing that they love and wanted to do and always wanted to do; they chose not to do it because they wanted to stay in a company they thought was loyal to them. Companies today don't have any loyalty to you, and honestly, they never did. Most of us are at-will employees. We work for an at-will employer. And what does that mean? That means that, at any point in time that the company gets ready, it will release you because it no longer needs your services.

And so, entrepreneurship is extremely important because you have an opportunity to create value for yourself, to create a legacy, to build something that can outlast and sustain in any time because it's yours and you know how to build it, leverage it and create it. And more importantly today, even education is changing, and the equivalent of a Bachelor's degree used to be valuable, and now you almost need a Masters degree to get an entry-level position. Being an entrepreneur allows you to be able to transcend those things the world says are important. When you work for yourself, *you* can determine what's important, and what's necessary, and what's needed to help you grow and sustain your life the way you want to live it.

Be prepared financially

Save 6-9 months or 6-12 months of your salary when you're working for someone else just for a rainy day. I remember scoffing at the idea of saving that much money because it seemed like a lot of money at the time until I became an entrepreneur. Even if you got a severance package with a layoff, for example, that money is awesome. But most people don't have the right mindset for money. And as a result, when you're an entrepreneur, you'll very quickly learn that everything you were accustomed to having access to in terms of resources in your organization, software, and tools, you now have to purchase yourself as an entrepreneur. You have to purchase Adobe products you need to create your design. You have to purchase the email list you're familiar with utilizing.

There's a lot financially that goes into being an entrepreneur to help you stand up your business, not just getting it started but maintaining and sustaining it. Finances are extremely vital. I do agree now that you need to have at least 6-12 months of savings, if not more, set aside so your family does not suffer, is taken care of so that you are taken care of and there's not a burden there that can cause you to lose sight of what you set out to accomplish. It will feel like you're losing everything if you're not careful, but you have to give up everything to make this dream a reality. And then if it doesn't pan out the way that you expect it to in the timeframe you expected, it hurts.

By setting aside an amount every month, start to leverage by purchasing what you need today while you're still employed. Set aside any bonuses. I do recommend tithing. If you're a tither, then return the tithe and save everything else. Only invest in things that will help you build your business, or your dream, or a specific reason. I recommend the following approach to save money: 10% tithe, 10% to yourself, 20% savings and then the rest is what your family uses to live and function.

How to get started

In the space of entrepreneurship, I used to coach people how to start their specific industry business. Now I refer people to their local small business development center. Every state has one at least. Usually, it's at a college, university or government entity.

I would start with what you want to call your business. Do some research. In Arkansas, the small business development technology center that typically is available in almost every community is a community resource, usually free, available to entrepreneurs. It's a free resource that you can use online. There are tools and resources available through the Small Business Association, or SBA. You're going to build and create a business plan that includes the name of your company, how much it's going to take to start that business, how much it's going to take to sustain it for at least a year, what resources you'll need, whether you'll have employees and so on.

A business plan will ask you some key questions. Who is your target market? Who is your audience? So there's a lot that's already available to you for free. I don't recommend spending a whole lot of money or investing a whole lot of resources on how to get started in business because there are free resources available.

You can take those free tools and leverage them and maybe get with a business coach, someone skilled at helping individuals start their business who will walk you through the legal implications for starting your business. I recommend an accountant to start with first because there will be some things you need to get started, like getting a Federal Employment Identification Number (FEIN), which is free. You don't have to pay anybody. You can get it yourself, or an accountant can help you. I do recommend having an accountant. I recommend having an attorney, too. You might look at prepaid legal services to get an attorney on retainer to help you establish contracts and agreements upfront so that as business comes, you're ready to engage in the business environment that's going to help you get started and get started well. Make sure you also look at your state and local requirements and policies, what is required there, and pay any licensing fees and necessary things to get that started.

Legal tips

I think are when you're first getting started, you'll need insurance for your business. A lot of people skip that. That's important. More and more I see companies put it in their statements of work or in their contracts that say, "Hey, at my event, you are required to maintain $XXXXXX of insurance. Do you have this insurance?" Even for just local vendor events, you have to have professional or general liability insurance.

There are companies online where you can obtain quotes. I won't limit it to any particular one, but the one that I use is *Hiscox.* They typically have been the cheapest I found, but you can also look at other services to get your contracts in place, especially if you're going to work with large corporations. They often have contracts available they want you to fill in, but you might not necessarily understand all the language. This is where having an attorney on retainer is helpful because they can review your contract. And you, of course, need to read through it but then to get their advice and to be able to say, "Okay, I don't like this language. How can I change it?" Or they might tell you it's standard or you may say, "Well I don't want to do business with them." So that's important.

Some additional considerations: Are you in compliance with your state or local government? That's important. And you are making sure when you sign an agreement if you have multiple partners that everybody's on board with how that partnership is established and how you're going to conduct business? Can you conduct business outside of your state? Or is it just within your state?

Get Your First 10 Customers

To get your first ten customers, there are several ways I've been learning from others in this space. Taurea Avant and *Show Your Success* talk about direct messaging. A customer can express interest on Instagram, for example, and if they follow you, you can use a tool called Instagood to actually have automatic replies and engage them in a conversation privately through direct messaging. And once you do that, you can get to the point where you can say, "I'm going to invite you to my webinar or my next workshop, or here's a copy of my book," etc.

It depends upon what you have available. One way to get your customers is through that. And in that example she shared with us in one of her coaching mastermind programs, I learned very quickly how effective it was. I saw her do it live. It was very effective, and that's how she got a couple of people even in the hour we were in conversation.

Another way is to hold a workshop or event and even if only ten people show up, you can leverage that to promote your services or products to those ten people. You can give away your services or products to the first ten people and then invite them to share testimonials or results from engaging with your service or product. You don't give it away for "free." They're not going to pay you for it, but you are, in fact, exchanging that for something in return, i.e., their feedback on how you can improve the program or service. And they can always have a sort of an introductory standard. "You're always a part of anything I'm doing because you're going to be my feedback team." So that's how you can get your first ten customers and start to spread word of mouth about your products or services.

Other ways include if you have a book. Then you can give away your book and provide your contact information for speaking engagements and opportunities that can then lead you to your first ten customers.

If you have a network marketing business, you can give away your card and a product you offer for free for individuals to try. The goal is to create an opportunity for people to try what you have for little or no investment initially and then leverage that to get in return their email address so you can build an email list, and then leverage that to communicate consistently over time when you're offering things. When you do, people will have a chance to see you're consistent and available. And they will come back to you or hopefully join you at your next event or engagement, or at least try your services for a discounted rate.

Conclusion

"You don't make progress by standing on the side-lines, whimpering and complaining. You make progress by implementing ideas."

—SHIRLEY CHISHOLM

CONGRATULATIONS! YOU MADE IT TO THE END OF THIS BOOK. We are so excited for you and the journey that lies ahead of you.

So here are some next steps. You've walked through each of these chapters, and there were some steps along the way. We started with you and got to know who you are. And you had to press into who you are and be willing to change. Remember Oprah Winfrey's quote, "There's no greater gift you can give or receive than to honor your calling." It's why you were born and how you become most truly alive that matters most.

I hope that as you've identified and recognized how you are most truly alive, you've identified what you like to do. You conducted the informational interviews. You've created an action plan that determines your next right step. You've invested in yourself. You've built the network before you needed it. You're ready to market yourself.

What's your next right step? That next step is perhaps a coaching discovery session with me. My contact information is located on the inside cover of this book. You might also be ready to sign up to take my course. So maybe the book wasn't enough, and you want to step into our career transition academy program where we will take the time to walk you through each of these steps with greater tools and resources than what we were able to provide in this book.

Other than that, we hope you'll continue to seek out resources to help you, to leverage your support network and of course, share this book with others via coffee for a friend, a neighbor or your team. You're also welcome to invite me in, and I'd be glad to come and consult with you or your organization, one-on-one or collectively so we can help you to move from a dead-beat job into a loving, fulfilling, joyful career that blesses you and others around you.

About the Author

DR. JACKSON WAS BORN IN MISSISSIPPI AND SPENT MUCH OF her childhood traveling due to being the child of a member of the United States Air Force. LaTonya enjoyed several higher education and corporate positions until she was met with an opportunity to D.E.C.I.D.E. her way forward. Ready to embrace a new and living way, she embarked upon the entrepreneurship journey where she discovered more than what she had ever hoped. The result was a process that lead to her learning to declare what she wanted, embracing a shift in her outlook on life and redefining success in the short and long term for her family.

LaTonya Jackson is an author, speaker, corporate trainer and career coach strategist who works with professionals to bring the unconscious conscious enabling their personal and professional growth journey's. LaTonya's research and experiences have shown her the power that lies in the discovery journey that starts from the inside out. The result is a life that is joyful, fulfilling and will attract to you the dreams and visions desired.

Her clients thank her for helping them to get comfortable with the uncomfortable enabling them to purposefully pursue their career goals and dreams.

LaTonya is the co-founder of Eyedentified Consulting Services, LLC, a personal and professional development consulting and coaching firm. She is a member of the John Maxwell Team where the focus is adding value and serving others.

LaTonya is co-author of a children's poetry book entitled *I Am Called*, with her daughter Sydni A. Jackson. The loves of her life include her spouse Maurice and their three children: Sydni, Josiah and Nathaniel. She also loves the beach and poetry.

If she can be of service to you or your organization as a speaker or coach, please contact her.

Info@eyedentifiedconsulting.com
www.eyedentifiedconsulting.com

www.ingramcontent.com/pod-product-compliance
Lightning Source LLC
Chambersburg PA
CBHW060253030426
42335CB00014B/1683